WAIT, REST, PAUSE

DORMANCY IN NATURE

~~~~~~

MARCIE FLINCHUM ATKINS

Ⓜ Millbrook Press/Minneapolis

FOR MY FAMILY—

who knew my stories would eventually bloom

〜〜〜〜〜〜〜〜〜〜〜〜〜〜〜〜〜〜〜〜〜

Millbrook Press™
An imprint of Lerner Publishing Group, Inc.
241 First Avenue North
Minneapolis, MN 55401 USA

For reading levels and more information, look up this title at www.lernerbooks.com.

Main body text set in Mikado a Regular.
Typeface provided by HVD Fonts.

Library of Congress Cataloging-in-Publication Data

Names: Atkins, Marcie Flinchum, author.
Title: Wait, rest, pause : dormancy in nature / Marcie Flinchum Atkins.
Description: Minneapolis : Millbrook Press, [2020] | Audience: Age 4–9. | Audience: K to Grade 3. | Includes bibliographical references.
Identifiers: LCCN 2018049345 (print) | LCCN 2018050487 (ebook) | ISBN 9781541561939 (eb pdf) | ISBN 9781541561922 (lb : alk. paper)
Subjects: LCSH: Dormancy (Biology)—Juvenile literature.
Classification: LCC QH523 (ebook) | LCC QH523 .A85 2020 (print) | DDC 571.7/8—dc23

LC record available at https://lccn.loc.gov/2018049345

Manufactured in the United States of America
1-46397-47487-2/12/2019

If you were dormant, you would pause—

WAITING,
RESTING,
HUDDLING,
CURLING,
NAPPING.

If you were a dormant tree, you would . . .

CHILL,

    REST,

        PREPARE.

In your limbs,
a sugary liquid would protect you
from freezing inside.
Tiny leaf blankets wrap around your buds.

You would pause.

In spring . . .

**DAYS LENGTHEN,
TEMPERATURES RISE,
YOU UNFURL!**

You would swarm into a ladybug pile,
sharing warmth together.

You would pause.

In spring you . . .
WIGGLE AWAKE,
FEAST,
FLIT AWAY.

If you were a dormant Arctic ground squirrel, you would . . .

PACK ON FAT,
BECOME AS COLD AS THE AIR,
BARELY MOVE.

You would pause.

Every few weeks, you shiver
for hours
to warm up.

As days grow longer . . .

**YOUR HEART QUICKENS,
YOU SCURRY AROUND,
YOU FIND FOOD.**

If you were a dormant chickadee on a cold winter night, you would . . .

COOL DOWN,
SLOW YOUR HEART,
SAVE ENERGY.

For just a few hours,

you would pause.

The next day you . . .
RISE EARLY,
REV UP.
YOU FLY!

If you were a dormant alligator,
when temperatures drop,
you would . . .

MOVE SLOWLY,
   BURROW INTO THE MUD,
   WAIT OUT THE COLD.

You would pause.

On warm days you . . .

COME OUT OF YOUR DEN,
SUN YOURSELF,
SEEK A SNACK.

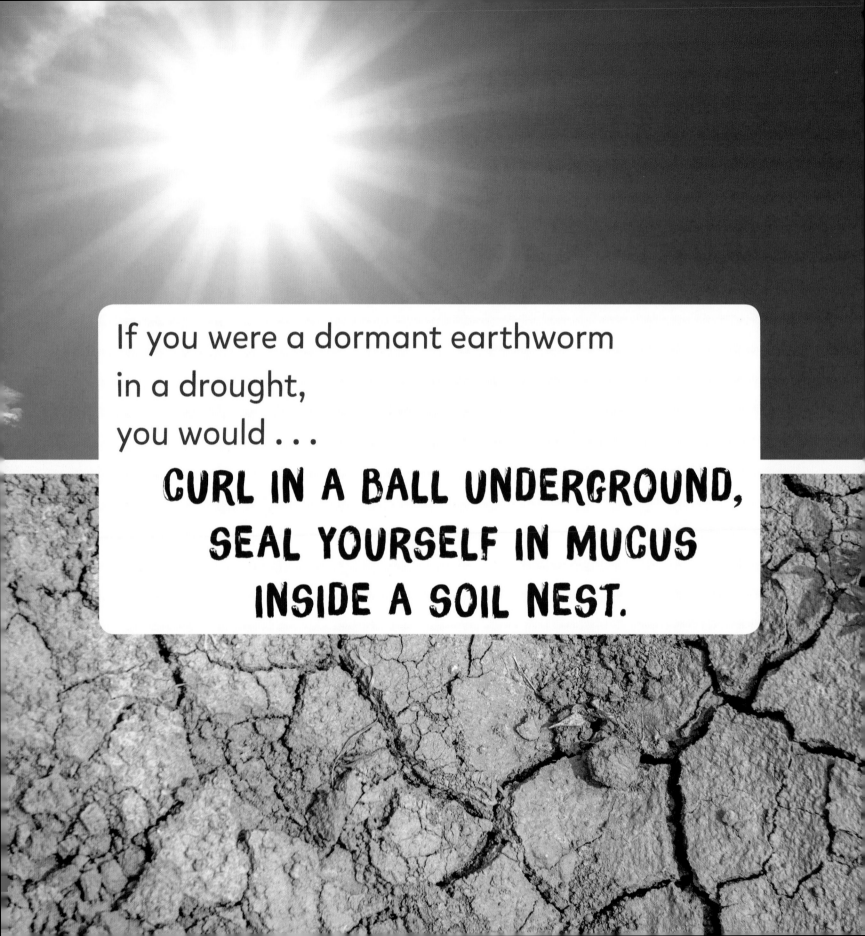

If you were a dormant earthworm
in a drought,
you would . . .

**CURL IN A BALL UNDERGROUND,
SEAL YOURSELF IN MUCUS
INSIDE A SOIL NEST.**

You would pause,

snug in a knot in the dry soil.

When the rains
return, you . . .

UNCURL,
MOISTEN YOUR SKIN,
STRETCH AND SQUIRM.

If you were dormant,
you would be . . .

silent,

still,

waiting,

just waiting,

until . . .

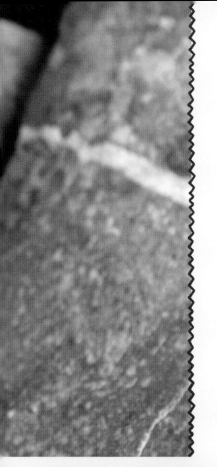

maybe the spring,

maybe the warmth,

maybe the rain

helps you . . .

STIR,
BURST,
APPEAR!

DORMANCY DIFFERENCES

During dormancy, a plant or animal stops growing and uses just the minimum amount of energy necessary to stay alive. Some animals can move in and out of dormancy, while others go into a longer state of hibernation. There are many different kinds of animal dormancy including hibernation, diapause, brumation, and estivation. Even volcanoes can go dormant. They may not erupt for years and then begin to spew ash and lava again.

PLANT DORMANCY
(plant DOR-muhn-see)

Did you know that both trees and seeds can go dormant? Deciduous trees lose their leaves when the days become darker and colder. These trees go into dormancy in the winter. The chilling that happens over the winter helps the trees grow better in the spring. But if trees wake up too early, frost can damage them. Seeds can also go dormant during a drought. This protects them from dry conditions that could kill them. They wait for the right conditions to sprout, and some may not sprout for a long time—sometimes even years.

DIAPAUSE
(DYE-uh-pawz)

Insect dormancy is called diapause. Insects can go into a state of dormancy in any stage of their life. Usually insects enter diapause as the days grow shorter and temperatures drop. Ladybugs (also known as ladybird beetles) start coming out of diapause when temperatures warm up, days grow longer, and food becomes available again, but each type of insect may have different conditions that force it out of diapause.

HIBERNATION
(hye-bur-NAY-shuhn)

Hibernation helps animals save their energy during cold weather. Their hearts slow down, and their body temperatures drop. An animal does sleep during this time, but some hibernating animals wake up for short periods. Bats, Arctic ground squirrels, and turtles all hibernate.

TORPOR
(TOR-pur)

Torpor is a short-term hibernation in which animals reduce their body temperature and heart rate to save energy. Birds might stay in torpor for a few hours at a time. Many animals, such as the chickadee, go into torpor during the winter. Many people think that bears hibernate, but some scientists believe bears actually experience torpor, or short periods of sleep.

BRUMATION
(broo-MAY-shuhn)

Dormancy in reptiles and amphibians is sometimes called brumation. Reptiles, such as the alligator, can slow down for many different reasons, including changing temperatures. Some alligators can even survive in icy waters by sticking their snouts through the ice and entering a state of brumation until the ice melts. Because reptiles are cold-blooded, they use the sun to help them warm up. On warmer winter days, they bask in the sun and drink water. Droughts can also force reptiles into brumation. Crocodiles, for example, dig a burrow in the side of a riverbank to rest during a drought.

ESTIVATION
(es-tuh-VAY-shuhn)

While hibernation happens due to cold weather, estivation occurs when animals slow their bodies during hot or dry weather. An earthworm does this during a drought. Animals may only need to enter estivation until the weather changes, such as rains coming or temperatures cooling a bit. Estivation helps animals conserve their body fluids and save energy. Animals including mosquitoes, land crabs, tortoises, worms, and salamanders can all go through estivation. (Note: Estivation is sometimes spelled aestivation.)

FURTHER READING

BOOKS

Arnold, Caroline. *Too Hot? Too Cold? Keeping Body Temperature Just Right.* Watertown, MA: Charlesbridge, 2013. Take a look at how humans and other animals keep their body temperature just right.

Posada, Mia. *Summer Green to Autumn Gold: Uncovering Leaves' Hidden Colors.* Minneapolis: Millbrook Press, 2019. Explore the science behind how tree leaves change with the seasons.

Salas, Laura Purdie. *Snack, Snooze, Skedaddle: How Animals Get Ready for Winter.* Minneapolis: Millbrook Press, 2019. Dive deeper into the world of how animals prepare for—and survive—winter in cold climates.

VanVoorst, Jenny Fretland. *Plants in Winter.* Minneapolis: Bullfrog Books, 2017. Follow along as plants respond to the changing season in various ways.

Waters, Kate. *Curious about Worms.* New York: Grosset & Dunlap, 2017. Learn more about how these squiggly creatures live.

WEBSITES

Animals—Ladybugs
https://kids.nationalgeographic.com/animals/ladybug/
Check out this website to learn all about ladybugs.

Hibernation
https://whyfiles.org/187hibernate/
Visit this site to find out some of the biggest questions scientists have about hibernation.

How Do Birds Survive the Coldest Winters?
https://wonderopolis.org/wonder/how-do-birds-survive-the-coldest-winters
Follow this link to see even more about how birds survive in cold winter months and get some fun tips on how you can help birds during winter.

Where Do Worms Go in Winter?
https://wonderopolis.org/wonder/where-do-worms-go-in-winter
What do worms do during the winter? Check out this website to find out!

PHOTO ACKNOWLEDGMENTS